Finding your VOICE Amid the Trauma and Drama of Everyday Life

Nicole Myers Sheppard

Copyright page

Ordering information
Quantity Sales. Special discounts are available in quantity purchases by corporations, associations, networking groups.

Foreword: **Pastor Sara Conner**

Each of us is born with a unique vocal deposit. Throughout life: events, influential moments and adverse circumstances threaten to shut us up, shut us down and shut us in. The greatest disservice to the world is silence where a voice is necessary. Silence is the easy way out. Speaking the message within our heart takes courage. We must fight insecurity, resist succumbing to criticism and press forward in seasons of pushback.

In Finding Your Voice, Nicole Sheppard pulls you in like a sister having a heart to heart on her couch. Through her own adversities and discouragements, her triumphs and testimonies she encourages you to take your finger off the mute button in your life and turn up the volume. Her rich experience as a professional counselor adds a great layer of practicality and insight.

This is a great subject to tackle. I am confident the lessons woven into each page will become a beautiful tapestry for all the world to not only see but also hear.

Sara Conner

Assistant Pastor Word of Truth

Arlington, Texas

Living to Give | Sara

Table of Contents

Contents

Dedication

This book is dedicated to my children: Michael, Anyae and Aniya Sheppard who are the loves of my life. To Dr. Michael Sheppard who has shared this journey of matrimony, child-rearing, vocal discovery and pursuit of my dreams with me.

To my parents who have continually etched resiliency within the fibers of my being by eloquently giving me courage to face my giants and to be confident and bold no matter what.

To all the people who have listened to my voice and helped me to share it and helped me to hear it as well, I thank you.

I have finally discovered my vocal strength, power and its innate ability to resound all over the world through my unique expression of transparency, vulnerability and authenticity.

To those who are in the midst of finding your own voice, I encourage you to continue the vocal work that is necessary to gain victory over every area of your life!

Introduction

As a woman, I find myself being a virtual hat rack. I wear so many different hats and each one demands more than the last. I'm a wife, mother, aunt, sister, mentor and friend. Those are just some of the hats that I wear and each one demands a significant amount of time, effort and engagement. Due to my having to wear so many different hats I often have lost my own voice and authenticity in the process. This book was written to women everywhere regarding the trauma and drama in their lives.

Over the last decade, I found myself increasingly swallowed up in the landscape of my life. As a mother, so much of my time is spent making sure that my children get a correct and right start in life. That means checking homework, mentoring each one so that they can become the powerful person they were designed and born to be. As a wife I've been supportive of my husband's practice, his career, and have attended to his needs. As a female in general there are requirements that we find ourselves encouraged to follow.

This book is not meant to bemoan or complain about the fact that being a female requires all these different hats. Rather it is a celebration of all of those hats and a blueprint of how to wear them and still maintain your authentic voice. In the midst of all the hats that I wear, the one that I seem to leave in the closet most often than not is the one called

9

me. My voice had gotten lost in the shuffle of having to speak and address all the needs that surround me. This book was written for me to find my voice and at the same time help you to identify and accept your own.

Our voice is a singular instrument that speaks to our potential, our purpose, and our path. When we lose that voice we lose our sense of direction. We find ourselves speaking loud and saying nothing. That is the thing that separates us and gives identity to who we are and what we can become. Recently my oldest child, my son Michael, graduated from high school. That required me as a mother to vocalize many things in order to ensure that his graduation and transition went smoothly. I am also the mother of a set of twin daughters that are the apple of my eye. But they too require a significant amount of my time, talent and treasure.

Each role that I've been privileged to accept is both a burden and a blessing. As a wife my role has been to support my husband and help him to identify everything that makes him both a man and a significant member of society. As a mother I relish my role of nurturer, confidant, encourager and healer. As a sister, friend and mentor each one means more to me than I can ever express. But it's the expression of that identity that is dealt with in the crossroads. As you read this book, you may see that your voice has been lost as well. You may find that even though you're speaking loud, the words that are coming out of your mouth are not necessarily those that are lifting up and expressing who you are.

Finding your voice in the trauma and drama of life is a significant task at best. Yet at the same time it is required in order for you to be able to scale up to the full potential of who you are. When you find that voice you will be able to perform each one of your tasks with more skill, power, and purpose. As you find your voice, it becomes incumbent upon you to help others find theirs as well. All the things that you find yourself engaged in are significantly impacted by the voice that you have. If that voice is weak, whining, and lacking the force that is within you, it will leave you voiceless.

When you find your voice you will be able to deal with and overcome many of the tragedies of life. The literary world is full of books that speak to your voice work and significance. Yet none of those will demonstrate how to effectively use it unless you have found your true voice. Journey with me as I share the five principles that I've learned, developed and utilized to discover my voice and to share that voice with the world.

Whatever it is that we're believing for, we look for confirmation from a human voice when it's our internal voice that we need to listen to and yield to.

NikkiSpeaks

Chapter 1: Validation

I believe that when you're searching for your voice amid the trauma and drama of everyday life, the first key principle of that is understanding validation. Sometimes, we look for the validation of man or woman to encourage us to step into the things that are pivotal to our success. We wait until someone says, "It's okay," and that we're worthy of the calling, the assignment.

Whatever it is that we're believing for, we look for confirmation from a human voice when it's our internal voice that we need to listen to and yield to. It's often challenging to do it on your own because so many times we want that support, that gentle nudge, that approval, that praise. We want our hands to be held through the process of cultivating our authentic self and voice.

Instead we should elicit the internal drive that we already have within us to be our guide. It should be our source of confidence, our boldness, our strength to move forward and embrace our true voice and purpose. Simply put, you have to believe in yourself, understand that you were born for a reason and are still here for the fulfillment of that contract between you and God.

Don't allow your self-doubt and the fear of untraveled territory prevent you from discovering who you really are. Validate your own voice by encouraging yourself that you can do it. Remind yourself of who you are by creating positive statements about yourself and who you want to be. Write down ten things about yourself that you love. If you have trouble thinking positively about yourself, think of your talents and strengths. What are the things that people consistently compliment you on, recall the successes you've experienced. Why not believe that the things you've accomplished can happen again even in your current situation?

Affirm yourself by telling yourself who you are through a different lens if you don't like who you are. You're in charge of your future and your potential to accomplish your dreams and goals. You have the ability to change the past you. You need you, it's a mindset you have to employ.

I remember when I was in the process of birthing my first *Voice Conference*, I wanted so badly for someone to validate me - to say yes, to say that they heard from the Lord that this is what I was supposed to do, this was my calling. I remember sitting in IHOP in Wichita, Kansas, with my Aunt Mini-Myers Card and I was going over the details of what I felt I was being led to do. As I was talking, she mentioned that she felt like she could tell that I needed validation, that I was seeking the approval of man instead of moving forward because of fear.

That really resonated with me because I realized that I wasn't listening to my intrinsic voice. I was looking to the human voice to see if someone could just tell me that this was what I was supposed to do, instead of believing and trusting in myself and what I already felt was my purpose.

I knew that the manifestation was necessary. No matter how much I doubted, it was that intrinsic voice that led me to use the keys on the keyboard of my computer to type out the plans for the conference. Then, the manifestation was necessary, it was the missing piece to so many who struggle with the concept of truly finding their voice through retelling their story. My conference provided a platform for others to be heard, their stories to be told and their lives as well as the lives of others to be impacted. I want you to believe in *yourself* today and to maximize your influence by saying "yes" to you.

You're good enough, great enough, wise enough, strong enough, and I truly believe that the validation lies within you. You have to accept that your voice is real. Your voice is authentic, it is unique to you. You've never heard of a successful singer who sounds exactly like someone else. That's because we all have our unique voices, we all have things that we need to say that can impact, influence and change the lives of others. We just have to be bold enough to believe it.

You can emulate someone else's voice, but it's still not your own. Stop being afraid to use your voice to inspire others and to make a difference. Stop looking at your flaws and worrying about what others think of you. When the viewpoint of others is shallow, you fall prey to their opinion and are in bondage to their desires for your life. You have to be willing to be yourself in the pursuit of your own divine purpose without anyone else weighing in as an imposter to your destiny. Your voice needs to resound among your circle of influence. It needs to be clear to others that you are called to inspire. In your sphere of influence, you're the only thing that's hindering you when you doubt yourself and the power that true vocal expression brings.

You also have to deny the naysayers. There will always be someone to tell you that you're not good enough. Why are you listening to those who don't have your best interest at heart? They serve as a distraction to the evolution and manifestation of who you are destined to be. Look at the fruit of their lives and how they've helped or hindered you in the past in various situations not just one time. You should consistently see support, words of encouragement and unbiased wisdom from the people who have "voice of reason" influence in your life.

That should determine their level of influence and gauge whether or not they deserve to have your ear. Some people do not deserve to have your attention. Their motive is to reflect on and magnify your past and imperfections versus highlighting the positive aspects of your character. This causes you to focus on the mistakes, problems, setbacks and misfortunes that life sometimes delivers with or without you co-signing on the trauma and drama that life brings. When someone tries to tell you who you are in a negative light, don't believe them. Use their slander, accusations and defamation as a catalyst to believe in yourself and soar beyond the low bar that they have set for you.

The night before I was to be a part of the panel at a conference here locally. I received an anonymous text that said so many negative things about me. I was thinking to myself, *"I would never do that to someone else."*

At first, I entertained the insults, but then I realized that this person was operating in their own hurt and disappointment. I let it go. You must let the comments and insults go. Completely surrender and let the false belief that their opinion matters go and set out on the quest to become the opposite of all that they use to attack you with.

Why is it that we listen to the noise of people who are not in our corner? They can't help us reach our destiny, but their voice can cause us to not reach our goals and dreams because we're too worried about what they think. We need to relinquish the right for them to have an influence, a voice, and exposure to our lives.

If it doesn't sit right with you and feels negative, release it. It's not for you. It will hinder the framework of who you are designed to be. Don't give power and a voice to those who use their mouth to tear you down behind your back. Ask God to illuminate the good connections and the people you are tied to that will help you progress beyond your

present circumstances.

Self-love, self-acceptance, positive self-talk, you're already equipped to move forward in the things that you desire to accomplish.

NikkiSpeaks

Chapter 2: Optimization

The next level is optimization, which is expanding your brand. You have to know that there is something in your belly, waiting to be birthed that was crafted and designed with you in mind. You have to be optimistic and open to the possibility of discovering yourself.

Self-love, self-acceptance, positive self-talk, you're already equipped to move forward in the things that you desire to accomplish. You don't want to abort your destiny, so don't stop before the manifestation of the real you evolves. You have to be optimistic and believe that it will be greater later. Be an advocate for yourself, encourage and exhort yourself. Don't minimize your influence or your voice. The world needs you, your voice and your testimony.

Leverage your platform, know your own worth, list your strengths, and all that you've accomplished. Write your dreams and passions in a journal or a place where you can reflect on them and use them as ammunition to surge forward and continue to move towards the manifestation of you.

How are your dreams, visions and purpose aligned with what you are currently doing? If they're not, then you need to search your heart and mind to determine what can be eliminated or added, so that your dreams can be accomplished. Positive self-talk is essential. We can all sit here and rehearse everything that went wrong in our lives. But what about all that went right, don't forget the good. A part of knowing your own worth is found in truly believing the best scenario for you. You must believe it to receive it and always trust in you.

What voice is magnified in your life, who are you giving full access and vocal contribution rights to? Are they for you or against you or do you know that? You also have to value who values you. There will be people who rise to the top to show you who they are, their true self.

Believe what you see. Everyone is not for you or assigned to your life. Even people from your past can show you their inability to serve you and be there for you.

Learn to not expect anyone to love and pursue your passion as much as you do. You only need to partner with those who truly support you. Find your dream team and value their input and contribution to your life and goals.

Pay close attention to the cheerleaders, who actually have facts and evidence to validate and support you and continuously remind you of that. These are the people who are pivotal in saying, ***"You can do it"*** when you think there is no way that you can.

Don't stop there. Validate those who validate and encourage you. Remember their names and support their pursuits. Be visible and present in their lives as you support them.

There was a time when I was going through a life crisis and I endeavored to reach out to a few ladies who I knew could help me because of their consistency in my life and because I knew they would be essential in helping me move to the next level of my dream pursuit. These ladies took me by my hands, cleared the path and illuminated it so that I could see which way to go. I wanted to start a blog, YouTube channel, enhance my social media engagement and write my first book. I had to let go and trust and believe that I have value and could do it.

You see sometimes you have to realize who's in your corner and who's not; celebrate those who are and remove those who are not. In order to fully optimize the people that are positive in your life, you must learn how to celebrate people that are celebrating you in a more intimate and proactive manner.

In order to celebrate those who celebrate you, you have to plug into their vision and be a part of whatever they feel they are purposed to do. You have to not only be a cheerleader, encouraging them and being positive even if it looks like it's not going to manifest, just giving positive words and feedback to encourage them to move forward and to continually pursue their dreams.

You just have to be there. You have to be present. You can't just be so focused on what your vision is, but you have to optimize those relationships that are formed or that are highlighted or magnified in your life. Collaboration is essential. Those partnerships where you know that you are destined to assist that person in the fulfillment of their purpose and their dream, their goals and finding their voice are priceless connections.

That's being a cheerleader, being present, being visible, offering the assistance that you are able to offer due to your talents, your skills, your abilities, and your financial contributions. Whatever it is that you need to optimize in order to benefit from the relationship, which is the connection, that collaboration, that mutual support and desire to see someone else make it as well as you. To see others be able to fulfill those things that they want to fulfill is an amazing thing.

Being free enough to balance and help them achieve their goals, which ultimately opens an opportunity for you to achieve yours. If you find that you are the sharpest tool in the shed, that you are the smartest in the room, is it not wise to stay there? I suggest going to another area where people are sharper, so they can sharpen you, strengthen you and make you a better person.

I believe that with dual partnerships, you have to be connected with those who are rising with you. I think there's something magnetic about that and something inspirational. There's that positive energy, a camaraderie among those who are aspiring to accomplish the same things.

Then, you also have to be wise to plug into those who have achieved more than you have in that arena so that you can gain from their wisdom, influence, connections and their resources. Seek out synchronicity in order to avoid becoming stagnant. You have to be with those who are trying to do exactly what you are aspiring to accomplish. You also have to be connected with those who have more than what you currently have or have what you aspire to have one day.

The word "optimization" means making it your best. You talk about living your best life and part of it of course is the circle around you, but sometimes, it's accepting, acknowledging and leveraging the best within you. Ask yourself what are some of the things that, as you're seeking to find your authentic voice, that you need to do in order to be your best self.

Moving forward, looking in the past and forgetting the lies that you have been telling yourself, looking forward and not being ashamed, fearful or feeling unworthy. These are all things that must be done to move in your purpose and being able to utilize the present in its maximum value, so that it produces results. From an optimization standpoint, how do you move yourself to a place where you feel confident that you are living that best life?

I think one of the things that hinders us the most is unforgiveness. Not forgiving ourselves, being too hard on ourselves, too judgmental, not allowing ourselves to make a mistake. We focus on the flaws, we focus on what hasn't worked, all the negative parts. I think with optimization, you have to look at those quickly and look at your mistakes or look at the pitfalls and the things that have not worked as a tool to learn or to gain advice for the future, but not for a place to stay. You have to move past that. I think with optimization, you have to forgive yourself. You have to completely love yourself.

You have to think outside the box and realize that a lot of times, what we share and when we find our voice, it elicits hope in other people and it gives them that ability to believe that if she did, I can too. I believe it's just that self-love, that self-acceptance and not being so overly critical of ourselves to the point where we become stagnant.

Often times we can become stagnant because we feel like, *"Okay, I'm going to do it, I'm going to find my voice, I'm going to discover my dreams and fulfill my dreams when I get good enough, after I lose weight, after I fix my relationships."*

It's all these *"ifs"* and *"whens"* that lead me to believe that sometimes with optimization, you have to just move forward from your current state. Forgetting the past, moving forward with a hope for the future. Positive reflection of our past is finding value in our ability to rise above it, good or bad. There's value in learning from the past, in analyzing it for how you can change for the future, not to fall into the same pitfall, but I don't believe that we should stay in that state of being focused on the past. We have to move forward. I believe moving forward encompasses us dreaming, encompasses us writing down our wish list because we still have breath in our lungs, we still have purpose and have to do more than hope for the future.

I remember at Christmas, as a child, I waited all the months of the year for that special day. I was so excited. I had the anticipation, excitement and joy as well as expectancy for the wonderful manifestation of my gifts. Likewise, we have to have that same outlook towards the future; that hope for that Christmas Day experience, which will be the manifestation of the things that we are working towards. The purpose is doing the things that are in our belly that we know we were called to accomplish and having that voice and speaking up for ourselves as issues come that we have to face and navigate.

Often, as we're headed toward that perfect place, that better place, that best life place, we find that it's difficult to navigate. It's difficult to get to where we're going because of the obstacles and the snags and just the stuff that obstructs us from moving forward with ease. I want to tell the person looking for their true selves, that there are three core principles that they need to focus on in order to get them the maximum self-expression they desire and the guide to finding their VOICE.

1: **Self-acceptance** Growing up, dealing with rejection issues from my past, I have personal experience with having low self-esteem and not feeling good enough or worthy enough. "I'm not light enough, I'm not tall enough, and I'm not smart enough." It's sad the power and significance that I gave to others instead of embracing the beauty in accepting and loving myself completely. I recall a time when I thought that I wanted to get all these degrees because I felt like, "Oh okay, if I just get one more degree and I have some letters I can put behind my name or I can have a title, I will have it all." I will tell you all that I am still searching for what it means to have it all.

I often thought, if I could gain more accolades I might be deemed worthy. Looking back now, I realize that I was so into hearing the validation from people and hearing that acceptance and approval from people instead of validating myself and optimizing my opportunities to excel. I feel like if I would have learned at a very young age that I have to love myself in my current state, flaws and all, I wouldn't have concerned myself with approval from anyone else. If I can love myself, truly love myself, meaning accepting my flaws, accepting what I don't have or what I feel the society feels that

I don't have, if I can just do that and say, *"You know what this is who I am and it doesn't mean I'll always be here at this level, but today, this is who I am and I accept myself."* Then I can move forward and discover my authentic voice. To me, that would be self-acceptance.

2: **Putting yourself first.** I feel like as a mother and a wife, I've always felt that those were my roles. If I have to work full-time, serve in the church full time and help take care of the kids and help with their education and all the things that are involved in being a mother, I was willing to do that. There's a way to do it, where I feel like there can be balance and just by being honest in saying, *"These are the* *things I can do, these are the things I can't do. I'm going to work on me simultaneously and I'm going to continue to pursue the things that I desire, so that I don't feel that I'm empty. I feel that I'm walking in my purpose and I'm fulfilling the desires of my heart."* You must prioritize yourself at the top of your list, but also be aware that you still have responsibilities.

3: **Not compromising.** Do not compromise who you are. A lot of times, I feel like I have personally compromised who I am because I've kind of cowered in situations and not spoken up because of self-esteem issues or feeling inferior. Sometimes I felt like I didn't deserve the platform to speak. I have discounted myself over and over again while failing to realize the value that is on my life. I may have been in a conference setting and I didn't have the confidence to go up and take the mic, even though the floor was open to us all to ask a question or to comment.

Because of me not feeling that I was worthy enough to speak, I compromised who I was because really I had a comment, I knew what I wanted to say, I had a question or whatever it was. I had to stop compromising who I am so that others felt safe and comfortable. *"I chose to minimize myself in order to maximize someone else."* A true statement of who I chose to be instead of being me. I believe we just need to be authentic. If the thought comes to you, you have to speak up and you have to have a voice. Even in dealing with arguments or disagreements, you have to have a voice in that. If your voice is not heard, then you need to take the steps to make sure that it's heard in a respectful manner, whatever that might be in your situation.

I

When people show you their true authentic selves, you have to analyze their purpose and place in your life.

NikkiSpeaks

Chapter 3: Introspection

Introspection means you have to look within to see what others see in you. So who do you allow in your circle? For so many years, I have been that person to always see the good in everyone. The person could be horrible to me and I would still find a way to believe the best for them. Over the years, I've seen a significance in and importance of selecting who has access to me and it has always been someone who is positive, uplifting and inspirational.

When people show you their true authentic selves, you have to analyze their purpose and place in your life. Have you given their voice the leverage to weigh in on decisions, even though they haven't encouraged you or been there for you in the past? You need to use what I call the ***Authentic Friend Gauge,*** to analyze the past to see if they have purpose to be in your circle and in your company. The ***Authentic Friend Gauge,*** is a gauge that you use to see how valuable, how real, how necessary a person is in your life. As you use it, you have to analyze it and see if a person is bringing value to your life. Or see if at this point in your life, if they are even necessary.

A lot of people want to get into your sphere, in your friend zone as it were, but a lot of them don't deserve to be there. The gauge will tell you if they are going to cause chaos, if they are going to be disingenuous or not the type of person that will lift you up or be able to help push you toward your goal. When you go into introspection and look at that person that wants to be in your circle, seek clarity and pay attention to the results.

You have to look at the evidence, the artifacts, like are you able to recall times in the past that this person has been a positive force in your life, has been a positive voice, and has assisted you in some manner. I think that the Authentic Friend Gauge can analyze the past with that person and be able to pinpoint somethings.

Of course no one is perfect. There are going to be times where they may not rise to the occasion or your expectation, but consistently, there should be a pattern there. I just believe that a lot of times we're so free with allowing people to have access to us and to our purpose and allow them in our circle, yet they're not necessarily contributors to the path that we're trying to tread. Sometimes, they are inhibitors or sometimes, they may plant a negative seed with their words.

You have to be very attentive also to the language that they use when they are in your circle, when they are in your presence. What is the pattern of their speech, how are they using their voice? Is it to empower or to uplift? Are they the deliverers of gossip and slander or defamation of someone else's character? Just pay attention.

It's not that you can't be social with that person, but anyone you allow to have close proximity to you should have your best interest at heart. If they're bringing other people's junk to you, then obviously, there is a possibility that they're doing the same of you to others, taking whatever you share and sharing that.

Let me disclose a little bit more in depth about the inhibitors and the contributors. As far as the contributors are concerned, you have those you can actually see have helped you or assisted you.

You have financial proof, you have the exhorters, those that encourage and uplift, that can contribute. You have those who are present, so they're there when you need them. They show up, sometimes even without asking.

Then, you have those that are discerners. They're able to pick you up, whether that be in the spirit or literal reality. They have a knowing of your present state and want to see you shift to that successful state, whatever that means for you. You may already be successful, but they want to see you go to the next level. Those are the ones you receive the call from out of nowhere, you just popped into their mind and they wanted to make sure that you were okay or they may speak into your life and authorize or speak life into the elevation they see regarding your future. Not that they have to, but they may authorize through friendship what you're called to do or destined to do. They kind of carry you through that way.

Then, of course, you have those who will pray for you and pray you through and those people, some of them, we will never know because they just pick us up in our situation and pray in secret for our best as intercessors and prophets and so forth.

As far as inhibitors, those are the ones that you may not realize it, but even in engaging in conversation with them, they plant seeds of doubt.

They plant seeds of worry or insecurity or those types of things into your mind to inhibit you from moving forward or fully flowing in what you've been called to do.

Then, you have those who will try to delay your vision. Sometimes that is surfaced through their own insecurities because perhaps they want to do something similar to what you've been called to do. They feel that you're already on the path to achieving it before them so they try to sabotage you or delay your vision by convincing you that you aren't ready, you're not perfect yet, you have too much going on or it is not planned out well. I will tell you from personal experience that sometimes God calls for a "quick work" in you.

Don't delay what has already been authorized and stamped with approval from the only source that can truly order your steps and guide your path. Yield to His voice and your own in all situations and circumstances but yield especially for those visions that require extreme faith and those that are too big for you to accomplish on your own.

Which leads me to the next one, those who try to compete, the competitors. They want to compete with you silently. They may be the ones that "borrow" your idea and never give you credit or acknowledgement for it. They try to discourage you from actually engaging in the completion of whatever it is you want to do. They also take what you have shared and create or emulate the same thing in a different fashion, but that looks the same, smells the same, is the same. Their purpose is to distract you or to kind of stagnate you. To delay what it is that you would like to do, so that they can be the first to do it.

Then, you have those inhibitors who are the false encouragers, maybe they're just nosy, but they rise to the occasion. They want to help, but they don't truly want to help. They just don't want to miss anything. They want to be around just to be present, but not necessarily to be an assistance to you and what you're called to do. The inhibitors aren't bad people. They're just not operating in the same vision and flow that you are because you have a destination that you're in pursuit of.

They can be the greatest people in the world and they may even be in your church, perhaps in your family, they may even be your close friends, but you just have to recognize that those voices, even if they are in close proximity, they have to be turned down. The volume on their voice and influence in your life has to be turned down.

The contributors are a part of your dream team. Your dream team is made up of those people who are pivotal in learning and understanding your vision and assisting you and walking you through that. Those people, they don't look the same, they don't talk the same. Yet they all have different parts to play in helping you to pursue your dream.

What I'm saying is that you have to look inside in order to see what's going on in the outside. You have to take into consideration that people can influence and impact you. They also can delay you, deny you and even destroy you because you're not looking at them from the proper lens, which is from the interior lens that sees how what they are doing in your life is impeding or leading your life.

Who do you allow in your circle? Do they bring value or steal your voice? These are questions that you have to ask yourself. Do they bring value or compete with you to have the same level of influence and impact in your community and nation? Sometimes, you have to be honest with yourself by letting go of anyone that is not aligned with your vision, or who you have been created to be.

So often, we want to compete for the level of influence that is already our own, you have to realize that the world needs you and your voice, your gifts and talents and your spirit. Stop being afraid to speak up for yourself. There have been so many times that I've accepted friends into my life, who fail to contribute on the level that I expected and needed.

I used to be upset with them because I didn't understand why they were not there for me. Instead they came to speak life into my insecurities or they stole my voice. Then, I realized that it was my responsibility to authenticate my own voice and to speak up for myself. If I didn't like it, if it didn't sit well with me or if it was not my portion, it's okay to say no to them.

I used to jokingly call myself the ultimate *Queen of Compromise.* You can't have a voice when you consistently compromise. You're giving into the other person's desires and not allowing your voice to be heard. Recognizing that positive contributions are a must in any healthy friendship/relationship is imperative.

You should have measurable evidence that the person is a benefit to having in your life. Over the years, I've been silent to even my own desires, often cowering down, fearful of speaking up for myself and lacking vocal substance and volume about issues that were important to me. When arguing with a family member or a friend or someone I would often *"let them win"* and I put that in quotation marks, even when they were wrong.

I was still operating in a watered down world of inferiority and failed to open my mouth to say what my true thoughts were. The times that I tried to speak up I inevitably would shy away from the conversation or argument as soon as I was able to detect that the voice was louder than mine. If you're like me, you don't like confrontation, so my compensation for my inability to speak up and over the voices that were louder than my own was to be the *Queen of Compromise*.

I would negotiate throughout the conversation, so the disagreement would take the backseat to our union. In my mind, I wanted to find any way we could to resolve the problem. If it took me taking the blame, that was better than going through the confrontation or frustrations involved with standing up for myself.

You also have to discover your Why, when you discover the Why and know the What, the How becomes apparent. Journals have been everything to me. It's what I've used over the years. I'm able to reflect on the past and review the details, set the scene at specific times that my sequence of life has dictated. How amazing is it to look back over pages of your written silent utterances and discover what you want and who you are and want to be? You have to search and discover your WHAT. I encourage you to look over all of your journal entries, listen to your voice memos, find your scraps of paper, your notes, even search within your phone and move forward in accomplishing the things you were destined to be and to do from the very time of your birth.

I promise you that if you take pen to paper, you will discover your Why and What and be led to understanding your How. I believe that your greatest dreams and the manifestation thereof are right at your fingertips. Your input and influence have already granted you favor. The resources to achieve the dreams and goals that you have are within vocal reach. When you know when, the universe conspires to help. Timing is everything.

Sometimes, we wait too long and sometimes, we don't wait long enough.

Balance is the key and definitely necessary. If you are truly connected to your purpose, you are able to visualize the fruition of your dream.

Finally, walking in your purpose and hearing the pattern of your own voice, the vibrations of your life experiences become apparent and you are able to find the assistance you need. It is like everything aligns when you surrender to the vision you have for your life.

If the goal is pleasing others, there will be times when we fail at that. Then, we have to walk in that disappointment of not meeting the mark.

NikkiSpeaks

Chapter 4: Clarification

Clarification is vital because you have to make sure you're doing what you are doing for yourself. Stop trying to please others. Do it for you, make yourself proud. Stop waiting for the pat on the back. You have to encourage yourself and not fall prey to the approval addiction, having people always tell you that you are capable, or to endorse the things that you want to do.

You have to make sure you're doing it for yourself and establish why you're doing it. Is your desire to influence? I know for me, I've always hoped to influence and inspire someone to be their best self. As a result of that I always try to make sure that whatever I'm doing, I'm assisting or aiding someone in getting the things that they need as well. Once I realized that it is most natural for me to help others, I've tried to keep that in the forefront of my mind so that I feel fulfilled in my work.

If the goal is pleasing others, there will be times when we fail at that. Then, we have to walk in that disappointment of not meeting the mark. When we make a decision to please ourselves more than anything, so many times we think that that's selfish because we're focused on ourselves. In order for us to fully achieve our life's goals, we have to stay in our purpose, which often requires a selfish mindset. We have to make sure that we engage in the practice of self-love so that we can also please ourselves, so that we continue to do the work purposed specifically for us.

Then, self-love and self-care are a vital piece of the puzzle. I have seen in private practice when counseling clients, that when we experience anything in life, the trauma, the drama of life, we often don't have that self-love, we don't have that self-care. That's the first thing we give up.

Not exercising and having a tendency to overeat or oversleep. Or we don't eat or sleep. We don't do things we're used to doing to take care of ourselves. Sometimes, I feel like it's self-sabotage, like we make our journey harder by neglecting the very things that keep us moving forward: self-love, which leads to self-care.

We also have to question whether or not we're climbing the right mountain. Even when you want the validation of others, you have to actually think about, *"Am I making the right move"?* What are you trying to prove and to whom? Sometimes, you have to take a step back and ask yourself those questions.

For me, I put an expectation on myself as a little girl because I felt like my story, how I came into this world was not perfect.

As a result of that, even as a young child, I started analyzing my life and I said, *"Everything that I see is broken within me."* As a little girl, I felt like I'm going to change that pattern by making sure that it doesn't happen to me.

Then, I wanted to be the first to go to college right out of high school. But that wasn't good enough for me. So I graduated high school a semester early and went straight to college. I was the first one in my family to come right out of high school and go straight to college and the first one to graduate from a university without going to work first and then, going back.

All these were pivotal moments for me, mental marks that I made for myself that I had to accomplish to achieve this American Dream. Where I received this American Dream, where I thought about this American Dream, where it came from, I don't even know. In my mind, I had painted a picture and I did everything that I could to accomplish what I wanted. I wanted to meet my husband in college. I met him in college. I wanted to have three kids. I have three kids. I wanted to get my degree. I have a degree. I even went back and got two masters degrees.

It took a refining moment in my career for me to ask myself, "Who did I do this for?" Was this really for me, was it for the approval of man, and was I climbing the right mountain? Even currently I'm considering pursuing my doctorate and I have to ask myself, *"For what, what is the purpose? Is the money that different? What will I gain?"*

It's all these things that we create and plan for ourselves or for others and as a result, we sometimes end up failing. All those aspects: my career, my relationships, my childhood, all those, even though I tried to create the perfect story, I still had human error. I still had failures, I still had trauma, and I still had drama. Sometimes it seems like if we do it the right way, which is whatever way we perceive or feel is right, then there's not going to be any problems at all. We won't have to face any mountains, we won't have to face our own failure and mistakes and we won't have to face any giants and that's not the case. We still have crises to navigate, we still have trauma and drama to endure.

It's just that sometimes when we're more centered, our mind is sounder. We know who we are, we know our purpose, and that makes us better equipped to navigate those situations in our lives because our mentality is different. We know who we are. We love ourselves. We know that we can get through it because we know who we depend on. We know that we have a dream team, that we have a core group of people because we use that

Authentic Friend Gauge and we can analyze ourselves, but not stay there.

We can look at the past, but not be so focused on the past that we can't move forward. When analyzing yourself ask yourself are you seeking to impress the wrong people? Who is your audience and why are they your selected crowd? I mean asking yourself that question, truly looking at the people in your lives that are around you and of course, not including family because you don't get to choose your family, but with friends, just analyzing that circle and making some adjustments as necessary.

There are people who are waiting on your victory from the sidelines as spectators in need of a solution to their own problems. If they can't hear your voice, they may not be able to find that solution.

NikkiSpeaks

Chapter 5: Elevation

Elevation is the process of moving up. Never stop striving. Sometimes, you will make mistakes and fail. Give yourself permission to be human and to disappoint yourself and even permission to disappoint others around you. You can't give up. There are people who are waiting on your victory from the sidelines as spectators in need of a solution to their own problems. If they can't hear your voice through written or vocal expression, they may not be able to find that solution.

If you can't do it for yourself, do it for your family. If not for your family, do it for those people who you don't know all over the nation, who need to know you made it. They need to hear your voice. They need to embrace your positive, resilient mindset, so that they can heal from their past and overcome their present in preparation for their amazing future. Their healing and victory is waiting on you. Though you may fail, fall and falter, get yourself up and try again. The world needs you.

Overcoming obstacles is one of the key components of elevation. I recall having a tumor in my pituitary gland when I was wanting to conceive my children. I had to go to the doctor and I found out that I had that tumor. I was so distraught because, I was the one that had planned my entire future and here I am in a doctor's office with an MRI scan of my brain and they're saying that not only do I have a tumor in my brain, but I may not be able to conceive...ever.

That was a divine moment for me because my mindset had to shift. I had to go into a mode of positive thinking, of building myself up because even though I was married, it wasn't something that my husband could relate to necessarily because even though he wanted children as well, it was my body. I had to fight that fight on my own and so that obstacle really strengthened me because it strengthened my faith. Also believing that I could make it on my own with positive thinking, encouraging myself through reading the Word of

God and standing on my healing and believing that the tumor was not my portion, but that having children was. That mindset enabled me to have three beautiful children. *"Your propensity to believe in elevation is very important to your life's success and essential in achieving and receiving exactly what you want in life."*

Sometimes when you're overcoming obstacles, there are many tears and doubt may creep in, not that worry and fear and anxiety are not present, but you have to negate those with positive thinking. If you feel like you're the person who has to overcome an obstacle, you have to focus more on the positive until you are only thinking thoughts that benefit you.

You have to confess more positive than negative until you're only confessing positive. You have to drown out negatives until the positive thoughts are the only things that you think of.

From that situation with the tumor, I was able to take medication for the tumor to dissolve and then, not only did I have one child, but two years later, I had twins. I had a multiple birth. It was standing on the Word of God, it was believing that I was good enough to have children and even though that's not everyone's story because I know there are people that aren't able to conceive. I believe that even in that expectancy, that hope and just knowing that you can be a parent and overcoming the obstacle and getting over the negative things that are present in our lives and we are challenged to face, we can still win.

Now that you have elevated, found the validation, optimized your whole purpose and you've done the introspection, so that you can see where you are going. Now that you've clarified and know exactly where you are, continuous education is in all the components that you are looking at and striving to improve upon. It means that you have to go back to school, seek specific trainings to continuously learn what the values are that you have for yourself, and how to utilize, strengthen and improve upon those values on a consistent basis. Continuous education is more than just getting the degrees. It's getting the core knowledge to live your best life and therefore, allowing your voice to be heard because people are waiting to hear it.

Continuous education does include getting the training you need to have your voice heard and also to fully develop your voice. Sometimes, you're not able to financially get that education you are aspiring to get, but there are always other avenues. Sometimes that comes through research sometimes that comes through having that core group of friends or family members who are able to connect you. That power of connection and collaboration, where you can maybe bargain or trade a favor for a favor, so that you are able to receive that continuous education.

Never be content with your current level of education, but always look for other opportunities and learn from them. When you are able to interact with those who may have the substance of what you need to be able to get you to where you're going, that's continuous education because you have to constantly seek those opportunities as the world continues to evolve and grow. We have to continue to stay on the learning curve so that we can elevate, so that we're in position to elevate, so that we have the knowledge and the experiences and exposure and the intellect of other people around us as well as our own to be able to go to that next level.

You can't lift yourself by pulling others down. That's so powerful to me because I think that sometimes we move into gossip and talking about people with the same voice that we use to encourage, exhort and uplift. We should refrain from using our voice to tear down and to highlight the negative things that are going on in people's lives because we too will have our opportunity to navigate something difficult. Life is never easy and we all make mistakes just in different ways.

We're all human and we all have to deal with hardships. If we have not already, currently, or if we haven't ever dealt with a particular issue, it may come in the future or we may have to assist someone else who we love in that process of getting through a major traumatic issue. We have to make sure that we're more aware of the way that we use our voice and the way that we influence others through the words that we say.

"It's not lonely at the top, just a better neighborhood." What I've learned from that, is that it's just not coveting financial blessings, we all aspire to get to the highest level of accomplishment, of financial gain with a positive light shining on our names. We all want that but then when you get there, it's tough because there's more scrutiny. Sometimes, people are more critical. The expectations are higher. The level of esteem is higher and so it becomes a challenge to navigate that, especially if you're not secure in who you are.

I love to shop, so I have a thousand clothes and shoes and it becomes an issue because what is the purpose of having all of these things? You may be put in the situation where those things could be compromised, all those things can be taken away. We have to, even as we elevate, stay in a level of humility and a level of awareness that it could be gone tomorrow and make sure that we are giving back just as much as we are receiving and helping others get to where they need to be in their level of success.

Then, success is a destiny, not a destination. Success belongs to you, is your portion and you can accomplish anything that you set out to accomplish. When you utilize the five steps of discovering your voice, I have no doubt that success is your portion because you will have an awareness of who you are. You will be able to connect the dots of your life and see that you can make it.

Why not you? So many times, we have all the reasons as to why we can't do this or that but we look at it from a negative light. But why not look at yourself in a positive light? Why don't you deserve it? *Just believing in yourself, connecting with those who are already doing what you want to do and asking them for help, you can get past your pain and find your own voice.* I have been touching on it throughout but basically being born into a relationship, where my mom and my dad were together, but then they separated and eventually divorced.

I struggled to have my birth father's attention. I struggled to have his affection, I struggled to have a relationship with him. Over the years, he and I would communicate, but it wasn't on the same level that I expected and it wasn't the level that he expected, but what we did was shift blame back and forth. I would call him and say, *"You haven't called me, you haven't sent me this, you haven't done this, and I haven't seen you."* He would call in turn and say the same thing. As a result, there was a feeling of rejection and that created a struggle between us.

Even though I had a great mom and a great stepfather in the home, it was hard for me to know that I had a dad out there that didn't want to have a relationship with me (or so I thought) to the magnitude or extent that I wanted to have. From there the rejection I felt flowed throughout many of the issues and relationships that I had in my life.

From there, it went to being involved in friendships/relationships I shouldn't have been involved in because I felt like I needed that validation, I needed that acceptance from humanity.

Although I received the love and support from my mom and step-father, I still wanted that intimate, close relationship with my dad. After years of communicating back and forth, I was able to have a wonderful relationship with my birth father and rejection became acceptance. However, many times over the years I began to seek affirmation and acceptance from others. Rejection came through issues at my job and issues with friends and family.

A lot of times, I would feel hurt, upset, and disappointed. Yet I didn't vocalize that. It took my birth father being on his deathbed a month before he died, I went to see him. He had a month to live and we shared a great conversation. One of the things he told me was to make sure, if nothing else, that I was happy for the rest of my life.

He surmised that if he could go back and change anything, that he would do that. Looking at the fact that he had only 30 days left and the only regrets were that he wasted too much time worrying, being upset, mad, sad, angry, frustrated, trying to get back at whomever, and that he didn't take enough time to enjoy everyday life, to be happy and to seek opportunities to do that.

When that conversation happened years ago, I began to trail blaze towards finding my voice in the pursuit of finding my own true self. It took a while to build my confidence up. I'm not where I want to be yet, but at least I'm closer than I was years ago. When I did that I started looking at so many areas of my life, it's almost like I had a magnifying glass. I had to search for happiness in every aspect of my life and I started seeing the missing pieces. I saw how the dots of my life, those pivotal moments, those peaks, those mountains, valleys, they weren't really connected. I started trying to piece them together so that I can have that happiness, that wholeness, that fulfillment from finding out who I really am and who I aspire to be.

Sometimes life experiences will cause you to not have a voice at all and you have to make certain that you don't want to remain the same anymore. You want to leave a positive mark on this world and impact those in your sphere. You want to impact it in the way that is uniquely your own, accept that, acknowledge it and move forward in it. That's it.

As a recap let me provide you with a powerful reason why every woman and man reading this book needs to find, identify and verify their authentic voice. Why it's so important that you use that voice and it's more than just speaking words. It's an identification of who you are, what you are, why you are and where you are.

If you don't, you will live, but you won't ever see the manifestation of what you are called to birth. What you individually are called to birth in this world. Your purpose, your voice, whatever magnitude that it's supposed to be, you will leave this earth without giving birth to that. It's like if you haven't had a child, and you have seen someone have a child, someone close to you experience that and going through the emotions from month to month as you plan, organize, and hope. You have all this joy with the expectation of the manifestation of this child and you go through that whole process and you get the fulfillment of that because you get to see that baby, but it's not your baby so you leave empty-handed. In a similar way, a life lived without birthing your purpose offers one choice: You leave this life emptyhanded.

It's important because there are people who need to hear from you and you're the only person they will be receptive to. I mean, there are millions of people in this world waiting on our voices to speak a word of power. We have to surrender even to our own desires of doing things our way and look at the bigger picture and see how we can help the next generation be better and the next generation to be healed and the next generation to find their way. It shouldn't take as long as it took for us. This shouldn't be as difficult as it's been for some of us.

When setting out to execute your purpose you may find it helpful to write down your desires, your vision. Do you see yourself helping young children, older people? Do the work and continue to elevate and the manifestation of your vision and your voice will come forward. Then, you can have complete joy because you know you're doing what you're destined to do. You know that you're called to do it and you're flowing in that.

I speak to youth, women and men who have lost their voice along the way and have been told their entire life what to do, so their voice has been hidden, extinguished. Now, in this book, I'm telling them to reclaim their voices. They look at the trauma that they face and the drama that they deal with on a regular basis and I'm saying that by discovering and recovering their authentic voices, they can overcome the trauma and deal with the drama and become powerful, self-expressive influencers and impactors in life.

My parting words are that *in my heart I want everyone: male, female, child, adult, and senior, I want us all to be able to have success in life and to find out who we truly are and not give so much power and influence and presence to our problems*. We should not amplify them to the point where it leaves us battling with depression, leaves us battling with insecurities and feeling not good enough or not worthy enough for the blessings that belong to us.

I believe that the strategies in the book, with the positive words in the book, will enable you to overcome those internal challenges. With a little effort in affirming yourself, believing in yourself and meditating on all the good, even if it requires listing out every good thing you know about yourself, you can achieve whatever is purposed for your life. I used to do this exercise with clients who struggled with self-esteem or depression. I would literally have them write a list, on the left of all the positive things they believed about themselves and the same amount on the right of negative things. We went over the negative things first.

I asked them specifically as we talked about the negative things, what's the opposite of that? That was showing them how they can change the way they think. We can think about the negatives all day, but acknowledging the opposite of the negative things and by focusing on the positive, we can work to change those things that we perceive to be negative. And there's power in that.

I had to do it that way too because a lot of times, I would say, *"Okay, tell me 10 great things about you."* You'd be amazed, I mean all ages, all ethnicities, and there were tears, all genders, tears. People struggle with affirming themselves. They struggled with being positive and loving themselves truly. They gave a lot of things about career. They would say that and I'd say, *"No, I don't want that. Tell me different qualities about yourself, your character, your personality, visually, what do you like about yourself?"*

Again, even with the career, so much is tied to accomplishment because we can see that as a landmark and it's important because that's where we're going. That's where we want to go. We want to accomplish things, but in the meantime, we have to make sure that we're also positive, we believe in ourselves and we love ourselves. So that when we achieve that accomplishment, it doesn't go to our head, we don't lose it because of mismanagement and we don't covet it to the point where it becomes our God or so important to us that other people are not. It's just a matter of really making sure that we focus on thinking positive thoughts about ourselves.

At a recent event called *"The Growth Experience"* I brought a young man up and analyzed his life. I did a laser focus on where he was based on past experiences. All of us have had, from birth to a certain point in our lives impact, influence and an immersion from outside areas, teachers, preachers, parents, other friends or peers. All of these influences impact us in a dramatic way, often drowning out our real voice and we begin to parrot the voices of those around us.

We begin to imitate rather than originate. The value of this book is that a person who has gone through those past lies are able to rediscover themselves and reemerge as a real authentic person capable of living their best life.

Once you have found that voice, now you have to find out how to use it responsibly. You do have to use it responsibly and be aware of when to use it and when not to because the goal is not to overpower or overshadow anyone. The goal is not to think better of yourself than you're supposed to, so you have to just be cognizant of that and wise when making sure that you're not abusing your voice. Do not use it to talk negatively to people or to talk down to people. A part of that comes from different situations and scenarios that you face and are exposed to. It's just about knowing when to speak up and when not to.

Sometimes life does require us to not be as vocal. I have found there are periods of silence that we have to explore because so many times we want to come to our own defense, but sometimes it's not necessary. We have to relinquish that right of having the last word or having a word at all, so that someone else's voice can be heard or so that it can be resolved a different way. Sometimes, in finding our voices, there's a bonus that comes, but that bonus needs to be made aware of when to use it and when not to and making sure that you use it the right way.

I'm glad we're at this point because now comes the punch. I say that **VOICE** means *Victoriously Overcoming Internal Challenges Effortlessly*. I want to unpack each aspect of that because that's the power of discovering that voice.

1: **Victoriously**. When you're victorious that means that you are a conqueror and that you win.

2: **Overcoming** means that you win and the obstacles put in front of you are something that you are not bound or stopped by.

3: **Internal** means that most of the conflicts, most of the things that are stopping you and your voice from being heard are actually internal conflicts. There's an inner fight, there's an inner challenge.

4: **Challenges** That word challenge. The challenges that we face, all the issues and the obstacles and the obstructions of life, these challenges that are not meant to defeat us, but to strengthen us so that we can actually become the person that we were designed and destined to be.

5: **Effortlessly** Finally, to look up and to see that all this has been done without effort, without restraint because the universe is conspiring to operate on our behalf and push us forward toward the glory and the dream that we have.

I would like to talk more about these elements here. Victoriously in finding your voice, I feel like we have to believe that we have the victory. For example, I used to run track and as I approached every race, I couldn't approach it thinking I was going to lose, I had to visualize myself winning and crossing the finish line before everybody else. Once

I got into those blocks, I had to tell myself, ***"This is my time."*** I just feel like this is someone's time who is reading this book to be blessed by this book because you've waited long enough.

You've waited to find your voice, you've delayed the process, but you have to forgive yourself and move on and realize that you already have the victory. Over all your situations, you have the victory and finding your voice is just one part of that victory. You have to have a victory mindset in order for you to be victorious. I don't know many people who are victorious that don't believe that they are or they don't buy into believing that they will be victorious.

Then, overcoming, believing that you're an overcomer. As you experience different things in life, disappointments or trouble with relationships or friends, you have to have that overcoming mindset that you are going to get past it.

There are so many times, where you may feel like you have a blindfold over your eyes or you have no idea how you're going to execute the next step, you have no idea what you're going to do next, but you have to trust yourself and trust your intuition and trust your faith and make strategic steps to prepare yourself for your future. Also, to repair those things that have been broken or those issues from your past. Believing you are an overcomer is very much a part of the success of finding out who you are and finding your voice.

Internally is where I believe the struggle with your voice happens because you can have a battle within yourself of appropriateness as to when to speak and when not to. So many things, your personality or maybe the things you've experienced in your past, you can at times feel internally that you don't have the right to speak up or nobody's going to listen.

You can have that negative self-talk and that negative mindset, where you convince yourself that you're disqualified from experiencing the blessings that your future promises you. You can convince yourself that you don't deserve it and that you are not worthy if internally you are battling with finding your voice.

That's why it's so important to have internally realized that you're going to make it. If you believe in yourself, that you're going to make it, then you can look to others that have made it and partner with them or have a relationship with them to see what they did, the steps they took to overcome their situations.

As far as challenges are concerned, you must have the realization that you will have challenges in life and just accept that. I think that some of us want to be perfect. We have this perfectionistic viewpoint

115

of life. If it's not exactly how we want it to be, then there's a problem. We don't want to deal with the challenges. We don't want to accept the fact that we're going to go through something.

As long as we live as humans, we're going to experience some disappointment, we're going to experience some setback and we'll experience the trauma, we'll experience some drama. Our goal is to figure out how to navigate it successfully, so that when we get on the other side of it, then it will assist us in moving into the things that we're supposed to move into.

In fact it should be done effortlessly, it shouldn't be hard. I think we make it harder than it is because we, again, focus on what we don't have instead of what we do. We often don't take the time to realize the importance of speaking up and if we have the mentality that it's without effort, that it's easy, then I believe that we're able to move beyond our current state and are able to the redeem the voice that the world needs to hear.

Afterword: By Johnny "Macknificent" Mack

Nikki speaks, and people listen. Often you may think your voice is unheard or the people just aren't listening. The truth is more people are listening and looking than you will ever know. Sometimes self-styled haters are looking at everything that you do, listening to every word that you speak and you don't even know it.

Other times family and friends seem preoccupied or caught up in the exigency of the day and yet they're listening too. Sometimes when it seems that no one is listening they're listening so intently that we miss it. It doesn't seem like they're listening because they look distracted or they look frustrated or they just look like they're not looking or listening.

The truth is people are listening and looking and they wonder how you have it together so much and always. Yes Nikki speaks and the whole world listens. Her friends, colleagues, her family, associates and people that she doesn't even know are listening every day. They listen by their actions that speak louder than words. They listen by the accolades that they share at golden moments that catch you by surprise. Yes Nikki speaks and people are listening.

As I begin to work with Nicole Sheppard on the formulation and creation of this incredible book I was struck with the fact that she felt people weren't listening to her. As I began to research and look at her life, I found quite the opposite was true. Her voice is loud and speaks volumes. From the two **"Finding your Voice"** conferences that she's held, to the children that she's raised that respect and honor her, to the many friends, colleagues associates and others that know her and respect her, believe me she is speaking volumes.

But what makes this book so special and so needed in the hands of women and men across the nation, is that it tells you how to find your authentic voice. She's been using hers for decades and she's found the right note and the right tone. As she shares with others how to look within and find that significant authentic voice it becomes evident that she is one of the true Visionaries and Pioneers of this time and age.

Her background as a clinical counselor bodes well as she looks into what is holding people back from voicing their authentic true selves. Is it the feeling of validation and self-worth that many feel they don't have? Is it the constant chatter from all around that drowns out our voice and makes it feel like its inauthentic or of no value?

Or could it be that they just have gotten so caught up in the narrative that says that they're not worthy that they begin to believe that no one wants to hear what they have to say? I dare to say it's all of the above. The most incredible revelation than anyone can have is that by reading this book you can find your authentic voice and as a result be able

to stretch and share your authentic voice in such a

way that it helps others to find theirs

About the Author

Nicole Sheppard, LPC Nicole Sheppard holds a Bachelor's degree from the University of Northern Colorado in English and Secondary Education and two Masters Degrees from Amberton University: one in School Counseling and one in Professional Counseling. She has eleven years teaching experience and eight years school counseling experience. She has gained a wealth of knowledge and experiences counseling her students and clients on various issues including self-esteem, bullying, anger, cutting, depression, rejection issues and coping with divorce.

In addition to her vast experiences counseling in the school setting, Nicole also has a diverse span of practicum and professional counseling experiences that include "The Parenting Center" of Fort Worth, Texas, "Epiphany Counseling and Associates" of Arlington, Texas and "Family First Counseling" of Mansfield, Texas.

Her counseling experiences outside of the school setting have given her the opportunity to work with clients and to develop a heart for counseling people who struggle with developing coping skills, establishing clear, attainable goals for themselves and those that lack motivation and focus for their lives due to the traumatic issues they have faced.

Her therapeutic desire is to lead her clients into discovering the tools and strategies needed in order for them to have a successful life. Nicole has spoken at a Multi-Cultural Christian Conference in Los Angeles, California and has been selected to speak at various workshops for teens as well as at church events.

Her love for public speaking has been discovered through her vast experiences in the school, church and community setting. It is her desire to see women, men and youth achieve complete restoration, emotional and mental wellness through life's situations and circumstances. Nicole was born in Tulsa, Oklahoma but spent most of her up-bringing living in various states due to her dad being in the United States Air Force.

Nicole and her family reside in Mansfield, Texas. She is an active member of Word of Truth Family Church in Arlington, Texas, a member of Alpha Kappa Alpha Sorority, Incorporated, President and Co-creator of a Non-Profit founded by her children called "Not So Basic Movement" which gives new and gently used tennis shoes to underprivileged children and founder of the "Voice Conference" which is a conference she birthed highlighting the lives of women and men through-

out the DFW Metroplex who are resilient and

successful in overcoming major life issues.

How to Contact Nikki Speaks

Email :

findingyourvoicewithnikki@gmail.com

FB: Nikki.speaks

IG: Nikki.speaks

Twitter: Nikki.speaks

Made in the USA
Las Vegas, NV
08 December 2021

36517518R00075